60 MINUTE GUIDE TO FABULOUS AGING

Live Long, Healthy, Happy and Young!

Admiral Dewey Sanders, Ph. D.

Edited by
Ann H. Crowe, Ed. D.
Phyllis S. Kramer, Ph.D.

DISCLAIMER

You know so well that **life has no guarantees.** You may do all the right things to be healthy and you still can develop a disabling or deadly disease. Conversely, you may even know someone who has lived a very unhealthy lifestyle but appears to be healthy into his or her advanced years. Yet, the most important thing to remember as you read this guide is that the healthier your lifestyle, the greater your odds are for living a long and healthy life. You already know through the media that heart and vascular problems, diabetes, various cancers, osteoporosis, COPD and dementia are often associated with aging. You may or may not experience one or more of these health problems. However, the more you make healthy lifestyle choices, the more you decrease your risk for experiencing any of the above health issues. If you cannot make a lot of the changes you need to make, even a few positive changes can increase the probability that you will stay healthy as you age.

REMEMBER AS YOU READ THIS GUIDE: You have been given the opportunity to choose how you live and it is a free choice with either good or poor consequences. You can choose healthy options that will increase your probability of having a long, healthy, happy and young life. Make unhealthy choices or no choice and you have significantly increased your odds of unhealthy aging. The choice is yours!
One very important reminder which will be repeated later in this guide is to never start any extreme exercise or diet without clearance from your doctor. When you begin making any significant changes to your lifestyle, always err on the side of caution.

Conflict of Interest Disclosure

The author of this book has no conflicts of interest to disclose. Author has no significant conflict due to financial benefits or support, other affiliations with commercial organizations, or any other people or groups who endorse this material. The mention of any group or business does not indicate that the author is endorsing any product or business but are simply giving examples or references for the point he is attempting to make.

FOREWORD

60 MINUTE GUIDE TO FABULOUS AGING obviously promises a lot in a short time, but can it deliver? In all candor, there are no guarantees because there are so many variables that can make your experience a success or failure. That is typical of most life plans that I have read or experienced. What is new is that I am going to share with you in a very brief time what I have gained from making healthy aging a primary interest. I have learned some strategies from attending workshops and reading the works of experts in this field. I have also learned from treating patients in a psychological therapy. I have had countless experiences over the years which have led to my beliefs about healthy aging. To say I am passionate is an understatement. Your writer is now 81 years old and extremely active doing those things we dream of doing "when we get old."

Healthy, happy and youthful aging does not happen by accident. It happens because we are willing to learn what it takes to age well, and then make the changes to achieve it. Science and the medical profession have found ways to keep us alive for a long time, even when we are sick and have no real quality of life. Who wants to live that way? All people want to live out their lives in a manner where they can enjoy the things they always wanted to do. If you are willing to carefully evaluate yourself and your lifestyle, you are taking the first step to a long and healthy life. Based on your self -analysis, if you can make some of the changes you need to make, you will begin traveling the road to health and happiness.

This small guide has both good and bad news. The bad news is that you will likely have to make some lifestyle changes, probably some significant changes. That is probably true for almost everyone who reads this book. The good news is that you shouldn't try to do it all at once. You should develop a plan through which you make the changes you need to make in an orderly manner. Try to do them all at once and you will most likely fail. Make a realistic a plan and you can work towards success.

So, for the next hour, read and make some mental notes of things you need to do to plan for a great life ahead. Then check out some areas that caught your attention as changes you need to consider. In the next week, start to make a plan as to what you feel are the areas where you need to focus as you begin. However, **please do not skip some of the preliminary things you need to do, or tests you need to get, before making too many changes.**

My wish for you is a life that is HAPPY, HEALTHY and YOUTHFUL to 100 years of age and beyond!

TABLE OF CONTENTS

INTRODUCTION

We live in a culture that is all about being young. George Bernard Shaw is often credited with saying that "Youth is wasted on the young." Young people live as if they will be that age forever with no thoughts of growing older. They are not alone. Aging is not a popular topic in our society since most people want to avoid discussing anything that calls to mind so many negative images. The prevalent ideas about aging in our culture make it the one phase of life that you would like to avoid. Is that true? Would you want to live to be 90 or 100, or would you prefer to skip old age or even die before you get there? You are probably in no hurry to die, but you may want to avoid the complications or changes that are usually associated with getting older.

To get a small sample of other's opinions, your author decided to do an informal survey * of 100 people to find out how they felt about living to a ripe old age like 100. The results were very interesting.

100 people were asked, "Would you like to live to 100?
- 51 said "no"
- 30 said "maybe" or "it would depend"
- 19 said "yes" if they were in good health and independent

*The samples were chosen from casual contacts by the senior author over a 30-day period of time. Responses were tabulated and grouped after 100 people had responded. The samples were not random as generally used in research. Why not? Why wouldn't you want to live to 100?

Reasons given included the following:
- Old people have chronic illness or chronic pain.
- Old people become disabled and dependent on others.

- They are miserable, unhappy and depressed.
- They have no fun in life because all their good times are in the past.
- Old people become poor and have money problems.
- Most older people are ugly, usually wearing clothes that are out of date.

100 people were asked, "Would you like to live to 100 without growing old?"
- 86 said yes
- 14 said it was a ridiculous or dumb question because 100 is old

So what is old age?

At what age would you say with certainty that someone is old?

- Historically it was believed that someone 65 is old and should retire. Yet you know people 65 who seem to be hitting their peak, people who are performing better than ever before.

- Is 70 or 80 old? It is certainly nearer the upper end of the life span, but again there are many people those ages who are still extremely active.

- AARP says that people age 50 are eligible to be members, but most people feel very young at age 50. In fact, life may seem to be starting over at age 50.

It has become evident that getting "old" is an individual definition. Some people get old very early due to attitude, lifestyle, injury or illness. Others, in more advanced years, seem young because they have followed a healthier way of living and have avoided the illnesses or injuries that are disabling. In the past century, retired people were seen by most people as being old. Today, people of all ages are retiring with many going on to a new adventure or job.

What do **you** think "old age" is like?

There are many views of aging but two are most prevalent. These include the traditional and contemporary views of getting older:

Traditional View
Getting old is a miserable experience and something you would like to avoid. There is nothing redeeming about growing old. It is just living out your days unhappily until you die with lots of aches, pains and sickness as the norm. This view believes the only good thing about growing older is that it is better than the alternative.

New View of Aging
There is a lot to look forward to and little to dread if we prepare ourselves ahead of time. It is a choice. If we make good choices, aging can be the best time of life.

What if it were possible to live to 100 and:

- Be independent, living on your own with minimal assistance

- Still be able to go out and interact with family and friends

- Be able to enjoy holidays, hobbies, food and entertainment

- Have good health; be pain free

Would you like to live to 100 under these circumstances? I would assume the answer for most of us is a resounding yes.

To check that out, 100 people were asked if they were interested in learning about lifestyle changes that could help them live to 100 in good shape. The results:
- 69 said yes
- 9 said yes, if the changes weren't too hard
- 11 said no; they were happy with their lifestyle
- 7 said it was all in the genes; changes would make no difference
- 4 said it wasn't possible; it was not a choice

IS IT POSSIBLE FOR MOST OF US TO LIVE TO 100? TO LIVE TO THAT AGE IN GOOD SHAPE?

IN THE PAST
In 1900, living to 100 was very unlikely as the average life expectancy for men was 47 years and less than 50 percent lived to age 65. This question would have been about something that people at that time would have thought ridiculous, unlikely to occur. People died much younger from infections, especially pneumonia, influenza or TB, all illnesses which today can be treated successfully with antibiotics. Childbirth was also a major killer in 1900.

In addition, quality of life was poor for many people. People knew very little about the importance of food choices, and in fact, the choices were often very limited. Sanitation and the opportunity for personal hygiene was very limited. Preventive healthcare or the thought of wellness was still in the future.

Today the leading causes of death are heart disease, cancer, chronic lower respiratory diseases, stroke and accidents. **Lifestyle has a significant effect on these diseases or events in many cases.** Get used to this fact:

LIVING TO 100 IN GOOD HEALTH IS BECOMING MORE LIKELY DAILY. It is possible, but it involves choices.

REALLY? IS IT POSSIBLE TODAY?

YES! And every year it becomes increasingly possible.

There were 72,197 people in USA in 2014 who were at least 100 years old, up from 50,281 in the 2010 census. (1) Over 80% of those people were women though the percentage of males is increasing. (2) Approximately 15% lived in their own home while another 35% lived with family. The rest lived in nursing homes/nursing care. (3) It is projected that by 2050, as many as 600,000 to 800,000 people 100 years old could be alive in America. (4) However, Ambrose Evans-Pritchard quoted Dr. Elizabeth Blackburn (Nobel Prize Winner in 2009) saying that people are alive today who will "have a chance of living to 150, and lifespans of 120 may well be the norm." (5) Whether or not these numbers are true, it does suggest that many people will be living longer. Just living longer, however, could be just existing. People today will want it all by living a long, happy life in good health.

WHY IS LIVING TO 100 IN GOOD HEALTH POSSIBLE FOR SOME AND NOT FOR OTHERS?

1. Some people have chosen a lifestyle that shortens their lifespan including:
   - Being a smoker; using tobacco regularly
   - Being obese
   - Being inactive or sedentary
   - Living with high stress on a regular basis
   - Avoiding regular health checkups
   - Abusing alcohol or other unhealthy beverages
   - Engaging in risky behaviors including sexual behaviors.

Reaching 100 in good health is also unlikely for some due to:

    2. Genetics
- Some people are born with increased sensitivity to certain debilitating diseases.

    3. Socioeconomic level of birth family or current financial situation often resulting in
- Poor nutrition, inadequate housing, poor healthcare

    4. Education/intelligence level
- Unable to learn healthy habits on one's own
- Unaware that they have a choice

    5. High risk or dangerous jobs

Unlikely for some, not for all!

True! Some people will live a shorter time or live with very poor health for reasons just mentioned.

Because of this and other reasons, many negative views of aging are driven by the media and popular culture that may be true for some but not for all older people.

What are these faulty beliefs? Many have called them the "Myths of Aging." You will note that these are the very reasons people gave for not wanting to live to 100. They felt that these conditions were an inevitable part of aging.

Myths of Aging

- Chronic illness; everyone is always sick when they get old.
- All old people become disabled resulting in dependency on others.

- Old age is painful; aches and pains are present daily.
- It is a time of depression and unhappiness; old people are miserable.
- Old people are all unattractive, lose their looks and dress poorly.
- All elderly people are crabby, irritable and negative.
- Older people end up in wheelchairs and nursing homes.
- Old age is a time of limited financial resources; most are poor.
- There is no fun in life and no enjoyable times for older people.

MYTHS OF AGING ARE MYTHS!
- These are myths that have been advanced by our media and our culture. They do not have to be a reality for most seniors.
- **Good news!** Even if someone gets sick, depressed or injured, an array of treatment options is often available.
- **Good news for you**! Start now to develop a healthy lifestyle and these myths of aging might never affect you.
- Most of these myths can be or have been debunked. The focus of this guide is on how to live long, happy and healthy.

WHAT IF YOU COULD?
- Live to 100
- Have lots of good days and good times
- Be reasonably healthy
- Be independent
- Have a good reason for living

You can, **BUT** you have to make those things a regular part of your life that help you get there feeling youthful, healthy and happy.

What keeps you healthy?

- **<u>Is it your doctor</u>?** Seriously, when did you ever go to a doctor to ask, "How do I get/stay healthy?" <u>NEVER</u>. You only go to your doctor when you are sick, except for a physical exam.

- **<u>Your health insurance</u>?** Are you kidding? You struggle to get help even when you are sick. Ask your health insurance to "Help me get healthy." They may have a token program, but that won't do it for most people.

<u>The TRUTH</u>:

<u>Your body and its healing systems keep you healthy</u>; and the better you treat that body, the more likely those systems will work for you. In the past, children were told in church that "the body was the temple of God; treat it well." Good advice for children but better advice for adults. You can start NOW! Learn how to keep your immune system healthy and make it work wonders for you.

When you think about aging, you have some big decisions to make about your lifestyle. To make those decisions you need to decide what you really want. Your choice will likely affect your outcome. With that in mind, what do you really want?

- To just stay alive to 100? Most people have already said no to that. You may also feel that is an undesirable option.

- To stay alive to 100 in reasonably good health and live independently? That is a good goal and one most people, including you, would accept.

- To live to 100 in good health with a passion to get up each day and live life to the fullest? Now that is a goal you can fully embrace. It is no longer just something for the few with great genes. It is available to more people each year including you.

As a 21st century person, you have the privilege of wanting it all. You can want to "live all the way to the end of the road" in good health and have a reasonably good chance of doing just that.

SIMPLE BUT HUGE STEPS IF YOU WANT THE BENEFITS OF FABULOUS AGING.

1. **Do not look for a quick fix!** There is none and never will be! If you really want to live a long, healthy and happy life, you will have to invest in some changes in your current lifestyle, at least most people will need to do that. These will not be short-term changes but changes you learn to live with over time. These are changes you get to choose based on how well you want to live as you age, but the most important ones will eventually need to be chosen and embraced. However, don't make all the changes at once!
2. **Take note of some things you should not do, or should stop if you are already doing them**! If you say you can't, you have already made your choice and you have likely chosen those consequences that are "the myths of aging."
3. **Use common sense to get good information before making too many changes, and take appropriate action based on information received!** This includes various examinations,

gender-specific exams, advice on diet, exercise and supplements.

4. **Do those things you should do to maximize health and wellness and make the lifestyle changes that seem most likely to help**! **Best advice:** Start doing whatever you can and commit to being successful with those changes. That will help you get started and may also make other changes easier.

Get started! A small beginning can have big results.

GUIDE TO FABULOUS AGING

THINGS TO DO BEFORE MAKING SIGNIFICANT CHANGES

1. Get regular physical exams with bloodwork and other relevant tests! Information is never a bad thing unless it is too late. (Don't ever say, "If only I had known earlier.")

There are some who say yearly physicals are not necessary. Since when is information bad? It is probably bad only for sources that pay the bill. If you can afford it, it may be wise to do even if you have to pay for it out of pocket.

You know that diseases detected and treated earlier are more likely to have a positive outcome. Get timely information! Your well-being is important. Physicals might best be done by a primary care physician or internist who knows you well. However, if your place of employment requires these physicals, their physician will suffice.

You should also have your **blood pressure** checked regularly since this is the "silent killer." You can feel great and still have problems. Lifestyle changes or medication can usually improve blood pressure problems. Even people in their late 30's or 40's can have major problems that can be corrected if they discover they have high or low blood pressure through regular monitoring and get treatment.

2. **Get regular gender screenings such as a prostate exam, PSA, gynecological exam, pap smear, mammogram plus other relevant screenings!**

    Again, information from these exams is good to have before problems occur, and regular screenings can help prevent major problems. You may well know several friends or family members who have discovered breast cancer or prostate cancer early enough to avoid serious consequences. You also may know people who had cancer that was discovered at a more advanced stage. Yearly screenings or tests can prevent the discovery of an advanced problem with potentially serious consequences.

3. **A colonoscopy should be considered by age 50, or before if recommended by your doctor.**

    There was a story told of a doctor who had a colonoscopy in his early forties to better understand his patients' complaints concerning the prep for these exams. His results indicated that if he had waited several years, he may have faced stage 4 cancer. A colonoscopy yields information that can save your life.

    Stories abound about people in excellent physical health who waited until their sixties for a first colonoscopy, only to discover they had major concerns including colon cancer. You can do all the right things with diet and exercise, but failure to get this vital information could have serious ramifications.

A diet high in fiber, plus regular exercise, can help prevent a lot of problems in this area.

Though a colonoscopy is not a pleasant exam to prepare for or experience, it can potentially save your life.

4. Ask your doctor to recommend a good multivitamin!

It won't harm you and it may supplement your diet, especially if you have not yet developed a sound plan for eating in a healthy manner.

You may also need to consider other supplements based on your bloodwork. This might include such things as a fiber supplement, vitamin D3, B12, probiotic or fish oil. Your doctor or nutritionist may be able to help you make a wise decision with this though getting good information on your own may also help.

Again, a good diet is always the first line of defense. However, in some cases, your diet may need to be supplemented and you can consider these other options.

5. Obtain good advice before starting any exercise program!

Consult your physician about any precautions to consider in starting an exercise program.

Depending on your physical condition prior to beginning a new program, certain tests or changes may be indicated.

Consider at least a few sessions with a personal trainer to set up a program to help you safely address your specific needs. These might include exercises to improve cardio functioning, strength, balance and/or flexibility. Initially it is a good idea to begin slowly and gradually increase what you do. Programs or classes through the YMCA/YWCA or a local health club might guide you as you begin. Also check with your local insurance company if you are a senior to see if it pays for the "silver sneakers" program.

Choose your exercise wisely as serious injuries can occur if you try too much too soon. For all of us, injuries can be demoralizing. Even with recommended programs like yoga or walking, begin with an easier activity before moving on to a more advanced one.

6. Consider obtaining professional advice in setting up a healthy diet!

There is an abundance of information you can access regarding ways to improve your diet. Countless books and diet programs advertise that they have the answer. For many, a session with a certified nutritionist through a local hospital might be a good place to begin. Though there are numerous weight loss programs, Weight Watchers is a good source of information because the program emphasizes eating fruits, vegetables and controlling portions of real food. There is also a good support system there for those who take advantage of it. For people who reach their goal weight and weigh in monthly within their goal weight plus 2 pounds, attendance at meetings is free. That is a great deal because you get free support for a lifetime if you choose. Other programs may offer similar benefits that work for you.

7. **By age 50, consider investing in a screening for heart, stroke and osteoporosis!**

    Several times a year local groups and churches will sponsor health screenings for a reasonable fee available at their facility. This is an inexpensive way to find heart, vascular and other health risks or problems before they become serious. As a rule, insurance companies and Medicare do not cover these tests, but they are worth the money if you can afford it. You do not need to have these tests every year, especially if you have regular physicals, but they provide excellent information you can share with your physicians as these tests may detect potential problems before they become serious.

8. **Throughout life, good personal and professional care of your teeth is extremely important.**
    Get regular dental checkups twice a year if possible. Infections that begin in the mouth can have serious ramifications for your health. Like other health tests, these cleanings/screenings can

help you prevent problems before they impact your health in a major way.

As you well know, you should brush your teeth and floss at least twice daily as this also helps to prevent teeth/gum issues that can affect your health in a big way. Use of a mouthwash, preferably without alcohol, may be recommended by your dentist or doctor.

9. Frequent hand-washing and regular bathing are extremely important.

This may seem unimportant to you, but it cannot be overemphasized. We have all been taught to wash our hands frequently, especially before eating. Yet in our world today, many people often eat, take medicine or otherwise touch their lips without washing their hands. After toileting or shaking hands with numerous people, you should always wash your hands. Sanitizers may help prevent the spread of germs, but good handwashing is always preferred. Also, regular showering or bathing is important, especially given the many lifestyles of people today.

10. Regular skin screenings are strongly recommended.

People who regularly play or work in the sun should begin to have skin evaluations by a dermatologist, possibly beginning in their early 20's. The same would apply to people who frequently go to a tanning bed. The best advice in this area is to avoid tanning beds or lengthy sun exposure. However, if you must be in the sun, always use a good sunscreen with an SPF of at least 30. Also consider using vitamin D if advised by your doctor.

You should note any changes in a skin growth, mole or other skin factors whenever you shower. To catch any skin problems early, the ABCD's of skin cancer are as follows:

1. Asymmetry: Moles or other skin growths should look symmetrical from top to bottom, side to side.
2. Borders: Border irregularities are a problem if they are blurred or jagged.
3. Color: More than one color, or black, blue, or red colors may be a problem.
4. Diameter: Larger than 6mm or a pencil eraser can indicate a problem.
   Skin cancers can be a major problem but caught early, they can often be treated. Do not ignore changes and have regular checkups!

SUMMARY OF THINGS TO DO BEFORE INVESTING IN SIGNIFICANT CHANGES

- Get regular physical exams with bloodwork!
- Get regular female/male screenings!
- Consider having a colonoscopy by age 50!
- Take a multivitamin if recommended!
- Get good advice before starting an exercise program!
- Obtain informed advice on a healthy diet!
- Consider investing in a screening for heart, stroke and osteoporosis!
- Practice good dental care with regular checkups!
- Wash hands often and bath regularly!
- Have regular skin evaluations to avoid cancer!

STRATEGIES TO NEVER USE

1. Never participate in a Super Weight Loss Program (one where you lose a lot of weight very quickly)! <u>Quick Loss = Quick Lost-Weight Regained</u>. These programs don't work because weight lost too quickly may result in weight regained quickly. These programs may be dangerous to your health because there is no quick and easy fix.
2. Don't get involved in an Extreme Exercise Program unless you are already in good shape! You will likely fail or get injured. It is difficult, and probably dangerous, to try to go from being out of shape to being Superman or Wonder Woman in a short time.
3. Don't use a pill advertised to fix everything wrong with you! If it were so great, advertising would not be necessary. No pill has yet been developed that can do it all.
4. Never depend on surgery to take care of problems you have accumulated through an unhealthy lifestyle! Surgery, including plastic surgery, may help some things, but it is not going to fix all the problems of aging.
5. Don't expect a quick fix because changes usually come through positive changes in lifestyle that take time to work their magic! You will waste money if it is spent on a wonder program or drug. Use this book or other good medical, nutritional or exercise advice to increase your probability of living a long, healthy life.
6. Don't get discouraged! If your inner voice isn't helping you out, Ignore it! **Remember this! There is NO EASY FIX**.

THINGS TO STOP

1. SMOKING: QUIT NOW! EVEN BETTER, NEVER START

Cigarette smoking is by far "the most important behavioral health hazard and preventable cause of death and disease"
facing Americans today" (6) Smoking is responsible for 480,000 deaths in the US yearly (41,000 of those because of secondhand smoke exposure) and the leading cause of preventable death. (7) "16 million Americans suffer from a disease caused by smoking." (8)

It is so obvious. Stop now or you have likely chosen very negative consequences. Smoking is not cheap, and it is a very good way to almost "guarantee premature, sickly old age" or possibly an unpleasant death. (9) Smoking is directly related to 40-50 different health problems including various forms of cancer, heart disease, COPD and stroke among others.

Be aware! Other tobacco use is not less harmful. Tony Gwynn, a Baseball Hall of Fame player, died in 2014 from cancer related to his use of chewing tobacco.

With almost one half million deaths from tobacco use yearly, **it is the #1 risk you can eliminate! Not easy, but others have done it. Believe in yourself and you can do it as well.**

2. BEING TOO SEDENTARY

People were created to move. Throughout history, humans had to move to eat and survive. Things are so much easier today to get food and live safely, but our sedentary lifestyle is deadly. We are eating more and moving less, feeling we have succeeded in saving steps. It is no big saving when our decreased activity contributes to early aging or premature death.

Not convinced? The problems related to a lifestyle that involves sitting too much or moving too little in our work and play include Type 2 diabetes, heart and vascular problems and weakness of legs and body. Also, as we age, falls often occur because we have become very weak due to being too sedentary. You don't have to be an exercise nut, but you must get up and move. Do what you are comfortable doing but keep challenging yourself to move and move more!

3. EATING JUNK AND PROCESSED FOOD

Junk = useless; so, junk food = useless food; even worse, it kills. Eating junk foods and/or lots of processed foods is easy to do as they are so readily available. Eating these foods regularly has a strong relationship to obesity. Obesity is deadly and kills almost as many people annually as smoking. These foods are everywhere and are invitingly advertised to make them look irresistible. They are not nourishing and can destroy your body if they are a major part of your diet. Interestingly, the more you eat them, the more you want them because of the additives in them. Literally, keep eating these foods and over time, you are likely to get sick or age prematurely. Worse than that, keep eating them and your health will suffer, obesity is likely, and you may possibly die earlier.

4. IGNORING UNCHECKED WEIGHT GAIN OR OBESITY

America (plus much of the western world) is experiencing an obesity epidemic according to many researchers. There is an overabundance of food at a time when people are less active or more sedentary. The amount eaten daily keeps increasing with larger portion sizes on bigger plates. Too many eat until they are full, way too full.

Obesity is defined as a BMI over 30 and people over that number are increasing rapidly, with 34.9 percent of U.S. adults in that range in 2014. Also, 18 percent of children and 21 percent of adolescents were reported to be obese and these numbers have more than doubled since 1980. According to the CDC, this has occurred because of a "caloric imbalance – too few calories expended for the amount of calories consumed." (9)

It has been reported that our increased food intake and decline in activity results in 300,000 preventable deaths each year. Heart disease, vascular disease and Type 2 Diabetes are all directly related to this epidemic. (10)

5. MAKING ALCOHOL, SOFT DRINKS OR ENERGY DRINKS YOUR DRINKS OF CHOICE

Alcohol: If you don't drink, don't start! If you drink alcoholic beverages, limit your drinks daily (1 for women, 2 for men <u>maximum!</u>); Resveratrol in red wine may help in preventing some diseases as people age, but resveratrol is also available as a supplement. It is noted that even one alcohol drink per day increases a woman's risk for breast cancer. (10)

Soft drinks: Read the label! Why would you drink anything where you don't recognize any of the ingredients? Drinking soft drinks regularly, even diet drinks, may make it more difficult to control your weight. There are some researchers who believe the diet drinks may be worse than those with sugar. Artificial sweeteners (such as aspartame or sucralose) may raise blood sugar levels and increase weight gain. (11)

Energy drinks: Have you ever heard anything good about them except in their own ads? A healthy diet and a good night's sleep do more for energy than some drink that is supposed to last several hours.

Caffeinated drinks: Coffee or tea with caffeine are best drunk in moderation, though their antioxidants make them a better choice than the above drinks. Still, most people should limit their caffeine daily to a maximum of 2 or 3 small cups.

As intelligent people, we need to **"think before we drink!" Water is your best choice** with 60-80 ounces daily recommended.

6. **IGNORING PHYSICAL SYMPTOMS OR CHANGES THAT PERSIST**

Symptoms = pains, aches, dizziness, breathing problems, vision changes, heartburn, bleeding, etc.

Changes are differences that occur with regard to your skin, toileting, sleep, senses or unexplained weight gain or loss.

All changes mean something and not all are bad. However, ignoring some can cost you your life. You should always check with your doctor when you have a question about some symptom or change in or on your body. Also, any persistent change that your doctor ignores but still concerns you deserves a second opinion.

A good suggestion is to document or track any changes (good or bad) daily in a journal.

7. **FEELING INVULNERABLE; YOU'RE NOT; NO ONE IS**

Teens feel invulnerable because they haven't lived long enough to know better, but many adults feel the same way. Every year in the US, more than 2 ½ million people die. Of those deaths, a large number was people less than 45 years old who were thought to be in the prime of life. (10) People die, and many of them may have felt it would never happen to them. Sadly, a large number of these deaths for both young and old could have been prevented. Though death is a fact of life for all of us, you can very likely extend your life and be healthy if you are aware of changes in your body or body functions. If you notice anything different, make a positive response sooner rather than later, and get it checked!

8. WAITING UNTIL TOMORROW TO CHANGE

Things we wait to do at some future time that can be deadly include stopping smoking, losing weight, becoming more active or getting a checkup. It may not be convenient now, but tomorrow will not do, because as you well know, tomorrow may never come.
Even a small change can help and might save your life. You don't have to be a health nut, but many small changes can save you money and help you enjoy life more in a very short time. Again, it might just save your life. RIGHT! YOUR LIFE.

9. LETTING OTHERS BE A NEGATIVE INFLUENCE

Don't allow friends and family to discourage your efforts to make positive changes! They may not be able to improve what they are doing, but they don't know what you can do. Believe in yourself even when others doubt! You can succeed! Young Ethan Bortnik wrote in a song, "believe in yourself and anything is possible."

Find other people who support you and what you are trying to do. Then use their support regularly since that is often the key to success!

A SUMMARY OF THINGS TO STOP

- Stop smoking, being sedentary, accepting obesity or big weight gain!
- Stop drinking the wrong drinks!
- Stop ignoring body changes without having them evaluated!
- Stop feeling invulnerable! You are not!
- Stop waiting for a perfect future time to start!
- Stop letting friends and family discourage your changes!

THINGS TO DO FOR FABULOUS AGING

1. **MOVE! This means you need to exercise but it doesn't need to be something extreme.**

In fact, whatever you do to move, you should begin gradually. If you were never an athlete, don't worry because this is not about becoming one. In fact, you can begin by parking further away in a parking lot or climbing a flight of stairs. Moving is about being healthier.
Any exercise must be something you enjoy if you are to continue it over a lifetime. You should remember to have fun with whatever you do.

Exercise (moving your body) is the #1 positive choice you can make to have a long and healthy life. "Physical activity is one of the most important investments you can make in long-term health and healthy aging. It has to be a priority" (13)
With the ever-increasing cost of medicine, this is the **best medicine you can ever take, and it is free.** It affects every function in your body.

Why not move/exercise?
There are lots of reasons people give for not moving, usually "I am too tired." Other reasons are disabilities, cost, work schedule, and time. Some may be legitimate reasons, but many are just excuses. Even moderate exercise will improve sleep and reduce fatigue. Better yet, you will be going in the right direction.

Know this! It doesn't have to be extreme, but you must begin somewhere, sometime. Wheelchair athletes in marathons are admired, but all had to start by overcoming big obstacles. Moving or exercise can be free such as walking in a park, mall or your neighborhood. It doesn't need to be in a gym. You can even buy instructional DVDs to help you begin moving at home, so people don't see you if this is holding you back.

You can join a class for yoga, Pilates, spinning, Zumba, line dancing, jazzercise or a variety of other activities. The options are endless.

Remember this! Begin easy and increase gradually but BEGIN!

More than anything else you can do, this will help you live a longer and healthier life because, as indicated above, it is the **#1 positive change you can make.** Once you are healthier, the guarantee is that you will be much happier as well.

2. EAT TO LIVE!

If you live to eat, you may die trying. What you eat, the amount you eat and your weight are all closely related to health and longevity. You, like many Americans (westerners), may need to make changes including:

- Stop eating fast food!
- Decrease salt, sugar and additives like MSG!
- Avoid saturated fats and trans fats!
- Reduce portion sizes! Seriously reduce portion sizes every meal!
- Eat fruits, vegetables and whole grains as the main part of your diet!
- Reduce red meat; substitute chicken, turkey or vegan dishes!
- Eat fish at least 1- 2 times per week (not fried)!
- Think organic! Wash all vegetables and fruit well!
- Make sure to get enough fiber daily!
- Avoid eating margarine! Eat butter only in moderation! Try grapeseed or olive oil instead of vegetable or canola oil!

By having annual physicals with bloodwork, you

can check how well your diet is working. If your general health is good, your numbers are in the acceptable range and you have good energy, it can probably be assumed that your diet is satisfactory. However, by educating yourself and/or using the help of a nutritionist, most people can still improve their diets. Remember, unless your health demands immediate change, you need to give yourself time to make any substantial changes. The food you eat can save your life and prevent many of the diseases often associated with aging. The reverse is also true; the food you don't eat can save your life. Educate yourself on a good diet and make changes, at least some changes, starting now!

One thing healthy cultures practice is to stop eating before feeling completely full. The people of Okinawa are very long-lived and eat only until 80% full. If you do this, in 15 minutes you will feel full. (14) Also, eat slowly and you will usually feel more satisfied.

Allow **occasional** treats, special meals or even a "cheat day." Return to your healthier diet the next meal or next day! However, if you have a serious physical condition, any deviation should be checked out before instituting any change.

If you have food allergies, keep them in mind. Older people are now discovering that they are allergic or intolerant to foods such as gluten, corn and dairy. Many have eaten these foods throughout life to their detriment. With this information, they can now improve their diet and reduce suffering. However, some of the symptoms of food allergies that may persist despite treatments that haven't alleviated them include headaches, joint or muscle pain and digestive problems. If you suspect you might have a food allergy or intolerance, get tested! Then take your doctor's advice seriously!

Plan ahead before eating out at restaurants, parties or holidays! You will enjoy yourself more by eating well without eating mindlessly. **Always eat mindfully!**

3. KEEP YOUR WEIGHT AT AN ACCEPTABLE LEVEL!

<u>What is an ideal weight?</u> The National Institute of Health has a chart listing ideal weight ranges for different heights. It also lists ranges for being overweight and obese. The Centers for Disease Control and Prevention also gives you tools for calculating your BMI with the understanding that a healthy BMI is between 18.5 and 24.9. A BMI of 25.0 – 29.9 is considered overweight while 30.0 and above is considered obese. <u>If you feel your BMI should be evaluated differently because of body build, consult your physician!</u> A BMI rating may not work for all people, but you should seek professional advice in evaluating your weight by a different standard. <u>Why is obesity bad?</u> Obesity increases the risk of coronary heart disease, hypertension, stroke, Type 2 Diabetes, cancer and respiratory problems to name a few. According to the NIH, "**obesity and overweight together are the second leading cause of preventable death in the United States, close behind tobacco use. An estimated 300,000 deaths per year are due to the obesity epidemic."** (15)
There are many reasons people are overweight or obese and not all are a lack of self-control. Many people try their best but have difficulty controlling their weight. Genetics, financial concerns, lack of information, health issues and unavailability of proper foods are reasons some people have weight problems. Other causes may include not liking to cook for one and apathy.
If that is true, how do you get your weight into an acceptable range?

The number 1 thing NOT TO DO is to follow a fad or trendy diet. There are no shortcuts despite their compelling ads. For people with other severe health issues in addition to weight, a hospital-based program where you are monitored by a physician and nutritionist is recommended. They can help you lose large amounts of weight and may even help you have appropriate surgery if necessary. One problem with some of these programs is their use of shakes or drinks in place of 1 or 2 meals per day. They will help you lose weight and get to a better level. However, you may not be able to do this for the rest of your life even though they work well on a short-term basis.

For people without a serious medical concern, follow a structured weight loss program based on real foods. It should teach you to eat in a healthier manner if it is to have lifetime benefits. In any weight loss plan, you should stay connected to people who support you. Additionally, it is important to keep your personal physician informed of your progress as you work any program.
However, you choose to control your weight, you must commit to the program.

4.   IMPROVE QUALITY AND AMOUNT OF SLEEP!

Sleep like you need it; you do. It is reported that at least one half of people 65 and older have sleep problems. This can include problems falling asleep, staying asleep, sleeping too much or a failure to get into a deep sleep. It can also include sleep apnea or other sleep disorders.

Things that might interfere with good sleep include caffeine, alcohol, nicotine, medications (prescription or over the counter), depression, anxiety, personal losses and exercising too close to bedtime.

A good habit to develop is having a regular time to go to bed and to get up in the morning. You should <u>not</u> make it a habit to go to bed and watch television. Rather, it helps to have a quiet time before bed for reading, meditating, praying or just relaxing. Your bed should only be used for sleep and sex. It also helps to have the room totally dark. Some people also seem to do well drinking some herbal tea or decaffeinated beverage prior to going to bed.

Reviewing your next day's schedule before bedtime to plan how you are going to deal with things on your calendar can be beneficial. It can help you to minimize stress by reducing worry about tomorrow due to any uncertainty.

Many people find it helpful to review the good things they experienced during the day. Being grateful for our daily blessings is good preparation for falling asleep. The Irving Berlin song was right saying "When I'm worried and I can't sleep, I count my blessings instead of sheep, and I fall asleep counting my blessings" (16) When you do this, you predispose yourself to having good feelings and to reduce negative thoughts before trying to go to sleep.

If problems persist, you should consult your physician. If any medication is prescribed, try to use it for a short time, not becoming dependent on it.

Naps work very well for many people. A short nap helps some people feel refreshed and ready to take on the rest of the day. It can offer the following benefits: improved performance, relaxation and increased alertness. However, even though short naps usually don't negatively affect your sleep at night, long or late afternoon-evening naps can interfere with sleep quality or going to sleep at night. (17)

Having a regular time to get up may have a positive relationship with the effectiveness of your sleep. Hitting the snooze button too often can have a negative effect on the way you feel during your day.

5.   NURTURE YOUR IMMUNE SYSTEM!

Living to a vital old age is increasingly likely if you keep a healthy immune system. Many of the stereotypical signs of aging are really the result of a weakened immune system. The autoimmune diseases such as diabetes, rheumatoid arthritis or thyroid problems are often caused by the immune system attacking instead of protecting your body. GOOD NEWS! There is real hope here. Mark Liponis, M.D wrote an excellent book on the seven steps we need to take to strengthen our immune system. He offers many things we can do to maximize our health and promote longevity. They make good sense and are easy to follow if we really want to live healthy for a long time. (18)

Some things he and others suggest to help nurture your immune system include:
- Eat to live! See suggestions made earlier.
- Get enough good-quality sleep!
- Develop good bedtime and waking habits.
- Reduce stress! Try mindfulness, prayer or meditation!
- Avoid taking antibiotic medications when possible! Regular use may reduce future effectiveness. They also kill good bacteria and reduce immune system functioning.
- Be active! There are many good choices including walking, sports, swimming or dancing. Just move!

6.   REDUCE STRESS!

Few people in our society live without a significant amount of stress. Peace is something we say we want but few find. Even very religious people who frequently hear about the "peace of God" fail to find it. We are stressed for many reasons including jobs, family, relationships, health/healthcare, finances and mental/spiritual issues.

Our society wants you to do more, quicker and with less resources. Work has become increasingly stressful and burnout is a frequent result. You work all day, then struggle to relax before bedtime.

Though stress is a major problem, there is no easy solution to correct it. It is important to avoid trying to deal with your stress through alcohol, drugs, or food. These are not a quick fix and tend to diminish your ability to deal effectively with stress.

Better ways to cope with stress include prayer, exercise, meditation, mindfulness, massage, yoga, chiropractic adjustments, music, hobbies and positive times with family and friends. More dramatic changes might include job change or counseling to reassess values, relationships or special areas of stress.

7.   STAY CONNECTED WITH FAMILY AND FRIENDS!

People who continue to have positive relationships with others tend to live longer, healthier lives. As we age, it often happens that we lose friends through deaths, moving or changing interests. Because of this, you should stay open to making new friends through work, clubs, church, volunteer activities and neighborhood. Flanigan and Sawyer say that "people who have satisfying marriages, good friends, and participate in religious or community organizations are generally happier and more satisfied, and enjoy better health and longer lives." (19) For whatever reasons, these connections tend to promote positive changes in your body that keep you healthier and happier, and will likely increase both the quality and length of your life.

Additionally, you should not just interact with people who are like you in most respects. Mary O'Brien says that the "superstars of successful aging interact with people of all ages." (20) When you interact with a variety of people, you tend to become more open and interesting. You are more likely to live with passion and positive energy which seems to promote better health and happiness. Increasing and strengthening social connections with family, neighbors, friends and even nature can help you live a longer, healthier life. (21) Even staying connected with pets or younger family members seems to promote healthier living.

8. LOVE YOUR JOB, LEARN TO LOVE YOUR JOB, OR GET A DIFFERENT JOB!

Job stress over time can be an extremely negative factor in causing you to age quickly and in an unhealthy manner. We strongly recommend that your career be something you enjoy or at least tolerate very well. If you cannot stand your job, consider a job change if possible. However, it is usually best that you not leave any job before you have another one. Being unemployed can be even more stressful than a bad job.

If you feel you must continue in a job you do not like to support your family, to keep benefits or because of age, it is imperative you find other activities you can look forward to when you are not working. This can be spending time with your family, working around the home, travelling in spare time, helping others less fortunate or doing a variety of other activities you like to do. These other ways to use your time may help you tolerate a bad job more effectively.

9. HAVE A PURPOSE IN LIFE!

People with a purpose live longer because they have a reason to live longer. A middle-aged woman was diagnosed with cancer and given less than six months to live. Her daughter was only 10 years old, but she decided to live until her daughter graduated from high school. For the next 7 ½ years, she cared for and encouraged her daughter. Two months following her daughter's graduation, she died having reached her goal. Her purpose had sustained her for all those years.

What is your purpose, your reason to get up in the morning? You can spend a lifetime looking for it and always feel you don't really know what it is. Every creature and every person has a reason for being here. Believing this, you can live each day to make the world a better place. By doing that well, you will come to know what your purpose is. The happiest and healthiest people tend to be involved in helping others whether it is your family, older people, children, the homeless, young parents or countless people or creatures in need.

To help you find your purpose, try to evaluate your talents, abilities, interests, values and activities. On your own, or with the help of others, seek to discover what you might do to make your life seem more meaningful or worthwhile. This search to find your unique purpose is one of the best things you can do for yourself and your health.

10. DEVELOP A POSITIVE ATTITUDE!

Flanigan and Sawyer report that "anxiety and depression have repeatedly been linked to poorer health and shorter lives" and "were associated with negative health impacts more than any other factors." (22) If you have become negative, it could be due to depression, **but** you are not having negative thoughts just because you are older.

Depression occurs at all ages and may be contributing factors to such disorders as heart attacks, stroke, diabetes or Alzheimer's disease. We know that depression is a mental health problem that can be treated effectively at any age.

What can you do if you feel you are down or depressed? First check with your doctor (one who embraces positive aging) to see if medication or counseling could help. Then, if you really want to improve, reach out to others (church, senior centers, local coffee groups) and generally get more active, more mobile.

Several studies have shown that positive people live longer. One study found that positive nuns lived an average of nine years longer. (23) How good is that? Some factors associated with a positive attitude include good social connections, marriage, positive self-esteem, an active lifestyle, a strong faith and a sense of purpose.

The Mayo Clinic Plan for Healthy Aging found that optimists tend to live longer than people who expected negative outcomes. They found that optimistic people were "77 percent less likely to die of cardiovascular disease, stroke or other cardiovascular event" even if they had a history of heart problems or high blood pressure." (24) We also know from personal experience that happy or optimistic people live more satisfying lives than their more negative counterparts. An important thing to note is that, like most people, you will have occasional feelings or thoughts that are negative, that is not a major problem if you don't dwell on them.

To develop a more positive attitude, it helps to deliberately focus on the good things happening to you, or in your environment. Be grateful for those things!

Gratitude has marvelous positive consequences when you learn to practice it regularly. By sharing your good thoughts and experiences with others, you will often find yourself feeling better. When negative thoughts come, it is often helpful to challenge them and force yourself to focus on the positive instead. Allowing negative thinking to persist often leads to an increasingly negative attitude with the undesirable outcomes cited above.

11. NURTURE YOUR SPIRITUAL BEING OR GIFTS!

Less than 100 years ago people appeared to have the ability to sit quietly and be alone with God, nature or themselves. People may have been more in touch with their spiritual needs even though they knew nothing about contemporary healthy living recommendations. Today, we are well-informed about the science of aging, but many have abandoned the spiritual components of aging as irrelevant. James Rippe, an eminent cardiologist, says that you can "nourish your spiritual age by participating in your place of worship or faith community, engaging in meaningful group studies, or taking courses in spiritual subjects." (25) You must learn to nurture the human spirit whether you try to find it in God, nature or somewhere else if you are to age well in body, mind and spirit. Perls and Silver report that "piety has significant protective effects for older people" and they often use it to deal with "illness, pain and infirmity of all kinds" (26)

What are some of those things you can do? Many people in the past were raised in the church, synagogue or some other formal religion. Others, even those who were never active in any formal religion, find real comfort as they age through a connection to God, the Creator of the universe or someone/something beyond themselves.

There is so much daily strength that you can access through prayer or meditation. The great thing about formal religion is that we can enjoy it in communion with others, or we can turn to it in times when we are alone. If you are a person whose faith is important, the Bible or sacred writings of your faith are filled with positive thoughts that you can turn to regularly for reassurance that life is good and that you are loved. Though these resources are not just for older people, they do seem to become a greater support in mid to later years.

Some things you can do:

1. Visit a church, temple or place of worship during a service, or even when no one is present!
2. Connect with people of similar beliefs!
3. Spend time studying scriptures or inspirational materials; pray daily!
4. Go to the ocean, forest, desert, waterfall, National Park or like setting!
5. Take time to be quiet, to meditate, to practice mindfulness!
6. Watch the stars, sunrise or sunset, take time to look at fall colors!
7. Pursue a big dream (not just a bucket-list item); e.g. walk a special trail! Set a goal!
8. Take time to visit/stay at a retreat/monastic setting!
9. Sit in a boat on a lake in the early a.m. or alone in the woods to watch deer, animals.
10. Listen to quiet music; contemplate works of art; read something to inspire you!
    Your opportunity, your decision.

12. COMMIT TO LIFE-LONG LEARNING!

Why would you ever stop? Yet countless doctors, professors and professional people stop most or all formal learning when they complete their degrees. Since knowledge is expanding at an unbelievable rate, you should always continue learning. Don't live on earlier learning experiences or you will end up like all those "old people" who bored you with their past lives! Though Alzheimer's Disease or other forms of dementia cannot currently be prevented, you can apparently reduce the risk by keeping an active mind. You can learn a new language, take up a musical instrument or pursue an area of interest with passion. People who continue to learn are happier, sought out as friends and have a sharper mind. Remember, people who are happier and more connected have been shown to live longer, healthier lives. Check out classes for seniors at a local university, the library, senior centers, nonprofit groups, AARP and Road Scholar.org! The benefits and rewards are great.

13. DON'T IGNORE MENTAL HEALTH ISSUES!

As discussed earlier, depression was previously thought to be part of growing older and therefore not a treatable age-related disorder. We know that is not true and that seniors respond well to various treatments for mild depression including medications and cognitive therapy. Depression is most common for people 40-59 and least common for people over 65 years old (4.5% males; 6.3% females). (27) If you feel you may be depressed, first discuss it with your physician (one who knows you are not depressed just because you are older). So many things including health concerns, stress, losses, weight or other lifestyle issues could be causing you to be depressed or anxious. There are medical and other interventions which may help. Remember that seniors respond well to treatment and can regain a full life.

If you feel you may be depressed or anxious, it is important that you and your doctor or counselor are on the same page regarding treatment. Conversely, you must be willing to work with them to overcome the disorder you are experiencing.

A big factor in any mental health concern is that you must feel some sense of control and believe that what you do will likely help you improve. There may be many reasons for the anxiety, depression or other mental health issues, but they can get better as you work with your doctor, counselor and other support people. Mentally healthy people live longer, happier and healthier lives, and you deserve that.

14. WHEN YOU RETIRE, GET A SATISFYING JOB OR FIND A MEANINGFUL VOLUNTEER POSITION!

The most important thing following retirement is to not allow yourself to sit down and do nothing. Sitting down is deadly. Unless you are sick, it is often a good idea to get a job or work that is less hours and less stressful than what you did in your career. It should be something you enjoy doing. It might be what you did as a career but with shorter hours and less pressure. It must be something you want to do. If it is a volunteer position, you should feel you are making a difference by doing your assigned tasks.

Keep this in mind! If you quit work and remain idle, your chances of dying earlier increase dramatically. Work all your life and sit down with the reward being

DEATH! Instead, stay active doing something. Many people today who may have a good financial retirement are still working a part-time job for extra income to travel, go to concerts, plays, sporting events or eat out more often.

Early in life, your job/work was often a four-letter word in the bad sense. You dreaded Monday and looked forward to Friday. In retirement, your job or volunteer position should be something you look forward to and feel blessed for the opportunity and health to keep doing it. An extra benefit is that you may find you get more respect from others because of your work or service.

A SUMMARY OF THINGS TO DO FOR FABULOUS AGING

- Keep Moving! This is your best free medicine.
- Maintain a healthy diet!
- Keep your weight in appropriate parameters!
- Develop good sleep habits!
- Nurture your immune system!
- Reduce and control your stress level!
- Maintain positive connections with family and friends!
- Love your job or find ways to make it be good for you!
- Have a strong reason to live!
- Keep a positive attitude!
- Nurture your spiritual being!
- Continue to learn and grow!
- Pay attention to your mental health!
- Stay involved in meaningful activities after you retire!

OTHER THINGS YOU CAN DO TO HELP

1. LIVE IN THE REAL WORLD!

Decide that you are not going to live in a fantasy world or the past. The real world is constantly changing, and you must go with it while holding fast to values and beliefs that have served you well in the past. That is often very uncomfortable as you age, but something you must do to stay relevant. In the 1960's, Bob Dylan (28) saw excitement in his song about "changin' times" even though some older people were resistant. The times did change and are much different now than they were even a few short years ago. Some were good, some not, but things are definitely not the same.

The world has changed more since the year 2000 than you may sometimes want to believe, but it is the only world you have. Remember, even smart phones did not exist in that year, but have only come into existence since then. Countless numbers of senior citizens use a current smart phone or tablet daily though younger people may use them more efficiently. You stay young by using whatever tools, knowledge or wisdom you have acquired in the past to live in a way that gives hope. You live healthier and happier lives by accepting the real but constantly evolving world, and using the opportunities and tools it provides.
Remember: Life challenges us to adjust to a constantly changing world.

2. THINK YOUNG!

This is not meant as a directive to deny your age, nor should you try to be a perpetual adolescent. Rather it is meant to act young by choosing to live each day to the fullest. You live by learning, growing, changing, adapting, planning and making new friends. You did this when you were young, and you must do this as you continue to think young.

Browning wrote in Rabbi Ben Ezra, "Grow old along with me, the best is yet to be." His attitude that the best is ahead as you age helps you to continue to live with hope. Regardless of your age, you can always learn something new that will change your life, enjoy the best moment of your life or even meet your best friend ever. As in your earlier years, there are still new experiences ready to be enjoyed and shared if you are open to them.

As you age, immerse yourself in those things that you always enjoyed or thought you might like to try someday. That can be the theatre, new sports, music, art lessons or doing new things to help others. Have something to look forward to each day, each week and in times ahead! Thinking about or planning new ventures is often enjoyable before you ever do anything. Remember: Think young, live young!

3. DON'T LIVE IN THE PAST

Related to the two previous sections, James Rippe encourages us to live in the present, not the past. (29) It is impossible to live in the 1960's, 1970's, 1980's (or any past time) because those days are gone. They may have been slower, easier, happier (at least in our memories), but they no longer exist. Truth be known, there were many struggles in those days as well, and those past times are not coming back. Live in the now and learn to enjoy the blessings you have each day. Also, remember how bored you were years ago when older people talked incessantly about the good old days. You need to realize that there are good times in all ages and you must learn to enjoy them and be grateful for your new experiences if you are to be happy. Life moves on and you must move with it or miss the many blessings life has for you each

day. The happiest people are those who find the good in each and every day they live. Best advice! Take 5 minutes each day to count the blessings you experienced that day. Practice gratitude! Your life will be richer and more satisfying. That's a guarantee.
Remember: Learn from the past, but do not live in it!

4. LEARN TO USE MODERN TOOLS

What is the worst thing that can happen if you really learn to use the internet, texting, some of the tools on your smart phone, smart TV or advanced security systems? Like so many others, you might like it or even get addicted. Nowhere has this been more evident than in available technology which can both make your life better and easier. For example, keeping in touch with friends and family through smart phones, texting, e-mail and Facebook is an improvement and cheaper than using the phone in the past. Travel apps can help you book rooms, find places to eat that are recommended by real people and suggest local attractions. Shopping on line has some risks but is definitely easier once you learn the basics. Things like Angie's List and several other apps can help you find reliable services. All of these things can make your life easier and keep you better connected. Yes, sometimes these smart electronic devices are frustrating, but they are worth the effort to learn to use. If you have a problem, you can ask your family or friends for help.
    Remember: You are up to this challenge.

5. PARTY HARDY (IN HEALTHY WAYS)!

Plan ways to get together with family, neighbors and friends on a regular basis, even daily or weekly for a social time if that is convenient. It gives you something to look forward to and affords you the opportunity to share the good things that are happening in your life. You know that shared experiences are better. Through such gatherings, you and others have a chance to keep a positive check on each other regularly for health or safety reasons. Life was meant to be enjoyed and good times with people you care about are the best times. An informal time for coffee, tea, your favorite beverage or a late afternoon snack with lots of stories and laughs can help lift your spirits. In addition, enjoy more parties (large and small) with family, friends and neighbors to enrich your life. Keep this in mind! If others don't plan these events, you can and should for your sake. Social interactions help you live longer, healthier and a happier life. You were created to enjoy the best life has to offer. Remember: You are important.

6. GET A PET

People are often reluctant to get a pet as they age for a variety of reasons such as pets are a bother, they tie you down and are an extra expense. However, research suggests that owning a pet may add additional years to your life. Why? The Mayo Clinic Plan notes that caring for a pet can help you cope with stress, live longer after a heart attack, improve mood, reduce loneliness and assist you in being more active. (30) These positive changes help you live longer and healthier. Judge and Wreden say that for pet owners, "one year survival rates after a heart attack were higher" than for non-pet owners. (31)

When you own a pet, you have to move to feed them, play with them or even walk some of them, but movement is good as indicated earlier. It gives you something to care for which is helpful, but you often get back far more love than you could ever give. When you are absent for one hour, most pets are as happy to see you as if you had been gone for a week. In our world, who else cares for us that way. As you age, you may feel invisible and unattractive to the world, but your pet still believes you are the greatest. Your investment of time, energy and money is returned many times over. Remember: You do not have to choose to live alone.

7. BEGIN A NEW HOBBY

There are many benefits to starting a new hobby, or even staying very involved in one you began long ago. To really enjoy any hobby, you must keep learning new skills as that provides a constant source of enjoyment. You also have something to look forward to on a regular basis as you research ways to enhance your hobby. Another real benefit is the opportunity to connect with others who have the same interest. Many people have learned that others who have the same hobby tend to be happier and more positive people. They are always looking to learn from or share some tidbit about their common interest. Dr. Joe Daugherty, an oral surgeon, was one such happy person who loved rocks. They were a constant source of pleasure to him, one which he eventually got to share on national late-night television. Remember: Find a satisfying hobby to enrich your life!

8. DEVELOP NEW SKILLS

Many people are trying to keep their "brain sharp" by learning to play a musical instrument or learning a new language. Accepting a challenge to go in a different direction from things you knew or did earlier seems to have beneficial effects mentally. This might also include learning to do such things as crossword puzzles, Sudoku or some new electronic game on your tablet. The options are endless but may help you keep mentally alert by moving in new directions. There are also other benefits such as making yourself more interesting to other people with the possibility of developing new friendships. It definitely helps you use time in a positive way as you can spend as much or little time on these new adventures as you like.

Remember: Boredom should never be an option.

9. LAUGH DAILY

One of the healthiest things you can do is finding ways to laugh daily. Using movies, books, TV, You-Tube or just being with others who make you laugh should be a regular goal. You likely have your own blend of humor that speaks to you, and you need to take advantage of that whenever you can. The bigger the laugh the better, for it seems to have some chemical reaction in our bodies that improves health.

"Norman Cousins shocked the medical community when he recovered from a life-threatening illness in 1964 using the power of laughter." (32) The Editor of the Saturday Review decided to treat his disease with laughter by watching comedy movies including The Three Stooges and the Marx Brothers. The result was more than 25 additional years of living, much of it in good health. He became an advocate for using "humor, faith, hope and love to help people heal and live longer." (33} This is one treatment for aging that costs little but may pay big dividends. One thing is certain. A close relationship exists between laughter, a positive attitude and good health.

Remember: Laughing is a very healthy choice.

10. MANAGE YOUR FINANCES

When you retire, the assets or resources you have acquired need to last as long as you do. With inflation, this is often a very tricky thing to do, but it is essential. Finances are a major stress for many seniors that can be reduced if you start saving early and control your expenditures. However, for seniors, the cost of health care and medications often rises significantly. Home repairs and yard work expenses also often increase for many seniors. Travel in retirement is expensive, but the cost for this is something you can control through careful planning. Things for the home, replacement cars and clothes are expenses that often decrease. To avoid unnecessary stress, it is a good idea to have a budget where you completely understand each month's income and expenses. The best plan is to stick to your budget and avoid impulse spending.

One of the most important things to remember is "where you came from in life." Many people have come from families where their parents always struggled to pay their bills. They did not get to enjoy yearly vacations, sporting events, eating out or concerts/theatre that you may often enjoy today. Gratitude for what you now have makes life happier even though you may not have unlimited financial resources in retirement, especially in later years. Remember: There is a difference between being thrifty and stingy. Learn to indulge yourself wisely! You deserve it.

11. GET A CHIROPRACTIC/OSTEOPATHIC ADJUSTMENT OR AN OCCASIONAL MASSAGE

For countless years, many people discounted the value of a chiropractic or osteopathic adjustment. Only recently have these come into acceptance by a majority of the population. Now, many health insurance companies will help pay for these treatments. Dr. Irvin Korr tells of learning the value of such treatments after the age of 50. He was challenged by a fellow professor at an osteopathic school to use the benefits of adjustments for optimum health. It must have worked well as he lived and wrote effectively to age 94. Having our body in proper alignment seems to be very helpful for maintaining good health.

Massages also seem to have a significant benefit for people who have them either to relax or to treat some bodily pain or soreness. People certified to do medical massage attest to the benefits they see for their clients on a regular basis.

The adjustments and or massages indicate that there are options to help relieve pain or improve health as we age, and these options can make life more enjoyable. Remember: There can be relief from pain or better health from a massage or adjustment.

12. WHAT ABOUT PLASTIC SURGERY?

People who have had plastic surgery have given mixed reviews of the benefits. For people who have had work on just their eyes, nose or neck, many have felt that it helped them maintain a younger look. For others who possibly expected too much, there has been a sense of disappointment in the outcome. It definitely is a matter of choice for every individual. Cosmetic plastic surgery may not increase your lifespan though some people may feel more positive about their appearance as they age. Some may also experience increased self-esteem or self- confidence after surgery though others may not.

However, where there is a need for plastic surgery because of an accident or illness, people should definitely have corrective surgery if they can afford it, or if insurance will help cover the cost.

Remember: Plastic surgery is a choice depending on your unique situation.

A SUMMARY OF OTHER HELPFUL SUGGESTION

- Live in the real world!
- Think and live young!
- Don't live in the past!
- Use the tools of today!
- Party hardy!
- Get a pet!
- Find a new hobby!
- Try to develop some new skills!
- Laugh! Really laugh!
- Manage finances!
- Get chiropractic or osteopathic adjustments, or a massage!
- Consider if plastic surgery is right for you!

WHERE DO YOU WANT TO GO NOW?

Given all the information presented, it is only useful if you apply it to your unique situation. You may now realize that there are things you need to do or changes you need to make. Are you ready to go forward with some lifestyle changes, or do you want to wait for some better time? If you have not decided you want to live and live healthy as you grow older, what is standing in your way? A partial commitment is better than no commitment. If you don't commit to making yourself begin, you may miss out on a healthier or happier life you could enjoy. **Remember that you deserve the best.**

Many older people today did not take good care of their bodies earlier in life because they were uninformed about of the negative effect of some aspects of their lifestyle. They often ignored new information recommending changes to improve health. However, many other seniors had an epiphany that they wanted to live and stay healthy as they aged. As a result, they made some changes and today are living very active lifestyles into their eighties and nineties. Their changes made a big difference and they are reaping the benefits today.

Remember this! You can't make all the changes at once and no one can. However, you might be ready to do something different because you care enough to still be reading this book. If that is true, there are some evaluation sheets in the following pages to help you get started.

To assist you in doing that, one other piece of information may help you develop your plan to improve. There are a few changes that may be more important or basic than others. These changes need to be a part of everyone's plan even though it is advisable to not try to do too many at the beginning. This includes the fundamental or basic changes listed below. What are the big things you need to do or the most basic changes you might need to make if you haven't already done so?

- Quit smoking! This is the #1 thing to stop.
- Move! Get some exercise regularly!
- Improve your diet and reach a better weight!
- Develop and keep positive relationships with others!
- Have a purpose for living!

Keep these basics in mind as you complete the four checklists that follow! These lists are meant to help you summarize areas where you feel you might need to make changes. They also help you see where you are already doing the things you need to do. Once you complete these checklists, you can make your initial plans as to where you want to begin now. Other changes may need to wait for a future time. Remember that your place to begin is unique to you depending on your lifestyle and current health. A physical examination might be a good place to begin. Your physician, family or a close friend can help you make your choices for beginning to live a healthier lifestyle.

1. **THINGS TO CONSIDER DOING BEFORE STARTING**

	DOING	NEED TO DO
Get a physical examination with blood work!	☐	☐
Get regular male/female examinations!	☐	☐
Have a colonoscopy (by age 50)	☐	☐
Consider taking a multivitamin!	☐	☐
Get professional advice before starting exercise program	☐	☐
Get informed advice for your diet	☐	☐
Have a screening for heart, stroke and osteoporosis	☐	☐
Get regular checkups for teeth with good dental care daily!	☐	☐
Practice regular hand washing, bathing	☐	☐
Get regular dermatological exams	☐	☐

2. <u>THINGS TO CONSIDER STOPPING</u>

	NO PROBLEM	NEED TO DO
Smoking; use of tobacco	☐	☐
Lack of exercise; lifestyle too sedentary	☐	☐
Eating too much junk or processed food	☐	☐
Unchecked weight gain or loss	☐	☐
Drinking too much alcohol, soft drinks or energy drinks	☐	☐
Ignoring any physical symptoms or changes	☐	☐
Feeling invulnerable ("never happen to me")	☐	☐
Waiting until "tomorrow" to begin making changes	☐	☐
Letting others influence you negatively	☐	☐

3. **POSITIVE CHANGES TO CONSIDER**

	DOING	ASAP	LATER
Get more exercise; move more	☐	☐	☐
Improve eating or diet	☐	☐	☐
Control weight	☐	☐	☐
Improve sleep	☐	☐	☐
Nurture immune system	☐	☐	☐
Reduce Stress	☐	☐	☐
Stay connected to family, friends	☐	☐	☐
Have a purpose for living	☐	☐	☐
Develop a positive attitude	☐	☐	☐
Nurture spiritual gifts	☐	☐	☐
Commit to lifelong learning	☐	☐	☐
Pay attention to mental health	☐	☐	☐
Get a job; volunteer; find meaningful work	☐	☐	☐

4. OTHER HELPFUL THINGS TO CONSIDER

	DOING	POSSIBLE
Live in the real world, the changing world	☐	☐
Think young	☐	☐
Refuse to live in the past	☐	☐
Learn to use the tools of today	☐	☐
Party hardy	☐	☐
Get a pet	☐	☐
Begin a new hobby	☐	☐
Learn to play musical instrument or learn new language	☐	☐
Laugh daily	☐	☐
Manage your finances	☐	☐
Get chiropractic/osteopathic adjustment or massage	☐	☐
Consider plastic surgery	☐	☐

YOUR COMMITMENT

With my assessment completed, I am ready to make a plan that works for me. I know can't do everything at once, but I will choose my starting point from the following things I need to do. I understand that I should choose only what is important to me. A maximum should be 3 things, but none is ok.

0 – 3 THINGS TO DO BEFORE MAKING MAJOR CHANGES
(e.g., physical, nutritionist, gender-specific exam)

1.

2.

3.

0 – 3 THINGS I NEED TO STOP
(e.g, smoking, fast food, sitting)

1.

2.

3.

0 - 3 POSITIVE CHANGES I WILL MAKE
(diet, exercise, weight loss, more social contacts)

1.

2.

3.

0 – 3 LONG TERM CHANGES TO CONSIDER
(personal trainer, relaxation program, learning program)

1.

2.

3.

MY PLAN, MY COMMITMENT TO ME

In 50 words or less, write your commitment to yourself on where you plan to start making changes to live a healthier lifestyle; then sign and date it! Review it frequently!

I WILL:

Signed:_____

Date:_____

BIBLIOGRAPHY

Agus, David B. *A Short Guide to a Long Life*. New York: Simon and Schuster, 2014.

Andersen, Wayne Scott. *Discover Your Optimal Health: A Guide to Taking Control of Your Weight, Your Vitality, Your Life*. Boston: Da Capo Press, 2013.

Anderson, Wayne Scott. *Living a Longer, Healthier Life: The Companion Guide to Dr. A's Habits of Health*. Annapolis, MD.: Habits of Health, 2009.

Bacon, John. *Dying Younger: U.S Life Expectancy 'A Real Problem.'* USA Today, December 9, 2016, p.3B.

Beare, Sally. *50 Secrets of the World's Longest Living People*. New York: MJF Books, 2006.

Blazer, Dan G. Ed. *Maintain Muscle Mass with Age and retain Your Independence: Muscle Strengthening, Aerobic Activities, and Good Dietary Protein May Slow Age-Related Declines in Muscle Mass and Strength*. Duke Medicine Health News, Volume 13G-R2, pp. 1-2.

Braverman, Eric R. *Younger You: Unlock the Hidden Power of Your Brain to Look and Feel 15 Years Younger*. New York: McGraw-Hill, 2007.

Broer, Ted. *Maximum Age Reversal*. Auburndale, Fl.: B & A Publications, 2003.

Buettner, Dan. *The Blue Zones: 9 Lessons for Living Longer from the People Who Have Lived the*

Longest. Second Edition. Washington, D.C.:
National Geographic Society, 2012.

Buettner, Dan. *Thrive: Finding Happiness the Blue
Zones Way*. Washington, D.C.: National
Geographic, 2010.

Byham, William C. *70: The New 50: Retirement
Management: Retaining the Energy and
Expertise of Experienced Employees*. Pittsburg:
DDI Press, 2007.

Capelle, Aleta, Managing Editor. *A True Best Friend:
Benefits of Pets*. Mayo Clinic Health Letter, June
2015, p.6.

Carter, Jimmy. *The Virtues of Aging*. New York:
Random House, 1998.

Creagan, Edward, Medical Editor in Chief. *The Mayo
Clinic Plan for Healthy Aging*. Rochester, MN.:
Mayo Clinic Health Information, 2006.

Crowley, Chris & Lodge, Henry S. *Younger Next Year
for Women: Live Fit, Strong and Sexy – Until
You're 80 and Beyond*. New York: Workman
Publishing, 2005.33

Crowley, Chris & Lodge, Henry S. *Younger Next Year:
Live Strong, Fit and Sexy – Until You're 80 and
Beyond*. New York: Workman Publishing, 2004.

Crowley, Chris and Sacheck, Jen, *Thinner This Year: A
Younger Next Year Book*. New York: Workman
Publishing, 2012.

Douglas, Sandra. *Anti-Aging by Choice: Easy Lifestyle Changes to Slow the Signs of Aging.* United States of America: 2012

Downs, Hugh. *Fifty Forever: The Complete Sourcebook for Living an Active, Involved and Fulfilling Second Half of Life – for You and Those You Love.* Nashville, TN.: Thomas Nelson Publishers, 1994.

Dylan, Bob (song). *"The Times They Are A-Changin."* 1964.

Editors of FC&A Medical Publishing. *Anti-Aging Super Foods for Seniors: 1001 Ways to Keep Your Belly Lean, Memory Sharp, Senses Keen, and Heart Healthy.* Peachtree City, GA.: FC&A, 2011.

Editors of FC&A Medical Publishing. *Fitness for Seniors: Amazing Body Breakthroughs for Super Health.* Peachtree City, GA.: FC&A, 2004.

Evans-Pritchard, Ambrose, *Telegraph.* January 20, 2016.

CDC Fact Sheet, *Fast Facts, Smoking and Tobacco Use*, Updated, March 29, 2017.

Flanigan, Richard and Sawyer, Kate Flanigan. *Longevity Made Simple: How to Add 20 Good Years to Your Life.* Denver, CO.: Williams Clark Publishing, 2007.

Flynt, Mike. *The Power Based Life: Realize Your Life's Goals and Dreams by Strengthening Your Body,*

Mind and Spirit. Nashville, TN: Thomas Nelson, 2010.

Forberg, Cheryl. *Positively Ageless: A 28 Day Plan for a Younger, Slimmer, Sexier You*. New York: Rodale, 2008.

Fossel, Michael, Blackburn, Greta & Woynarowski, David. *The Immortality Edge: Realize the Secrets of Your Telomeres for a Longer, Healthier Life*. Paducah, KY: Turner Publishing Company, 2010.

Fossenden, Marissa. *There Are Now More Americans Over 100 and They're Living Longer Than Ever*, Smithsonian.Com, January 22, 2016.

Fralich,Terry. *Cultivating Lasting Happiness: A 7-Step Guide to Mindfulness*. Second Edition. Eau Claire, WI: Premier Publishing and Media, 2008.

Fred Hutchinson Cancer Research Center, Communications@aicr.org, *New Report: Just one Alcoholic Drink a Day Increases Breast Cancer Risk, Exercise Lowers Risk*. May 23, 2017.

Gentzler, Jr., Richard H. *Aging and Ministry in the 21st Century: An Inquiry Approach*. Nashville, TN: Discipleship Resources, 2008.

Giampapa, Vincent, Pero, Ronald, and Zimmerman, Marcia. *The Anti-Aging Solution: 5 Simple Steps to Looking and Feeling Young*. Hoboken, New Jersey: John Wiley and Sons, 2004.

Graves, Ginny. *Cheater's Guide to Living to 100: 4 Super-Simple Secrets to Living Longer, Healthier and Happier – From Longevity Expert Dan Buettner and Centenarians Around the World*. Parade, April 5, 2015, pp.6-8.

Greene, Bob, Kearney-Cooke, Ann, and Jibrin, Janis, *The Life You Want: Get Motivated, Lose Weight and Be Happy*. New York: Simon and Schuster, 2010.

Greene, Bob, Lancer, Harold A., Kotler, Ronald L., & McKay, Diane L. *20 Years Younger: Look Younger, Feel Younger, Be Younger*. New York: Little, Brown and Company, 2011.

Gupta, Sanjay. *Chasing Life: New Discoveries in the Search for Immortality to Help You Age Less Today*. New York: Wellness Central, 2007.

Hill, Robert D. *Seven Strategies for Positive Aging*. New York: W.W. Norton & Company: 2008.

Howard, Michael, *Living to Be 100: 16 Common Lifestyle Characteristics of the Oldest and Healthiest People in the World*. Concord, CA.: Biomed Books, 2012.

Johnson, Lynn. *Enjoy Life: Healing with Happiness*. Salt Lake City, UT: Head Acre Press, 2008.

Johnson, Lynn. *The Healing Power of Sleep. A Guide to Healthy and Refreshing Sleep Skills*. Salt Lake City, Utah: Head Acre Press, 2010.

Judge, Kandeel, and Barish-Wreden, Maxine with Brees, Karen. *The Complete Idiot's Guide to Secrets of Longevity: Discover the Keys to a Long and Happy Life.* New York: Alpha Books, 2008.

Korr, Irvin M. & McGovern, Rene J. *Living Long and Loving It: Achieving a Healthy and Active Lifestyle.* Amherst, New York: Prometheus Books, 2008.

Lachs, Mark. *Treat Me, Not My Age: A Doctor's Guide to Getting the Best Care as You or a Loved One Gets Older.* New York: Penguin Group, 2010.

Levin, Neil, Kam, Jason and Qureshi, Irfan. *The Best Kept Secrets to Healthy Aging: Your Guide to Better Health and Longevity.* Plainville, N.Y.: Purity Research Department, 2009.

Liebman, Bonnie. *The Changing American Diet: A Report Card.* Nutrition Action Health Letter, October 2016, pp.8-9.

Liponis, Mark. *Ultra-Longevity: The Seven Step Program for a Younger, Healthier You.* New York: Little, Brown and Company, 2007.

Macnair, Trisha with Calof, Olga, *The Long Life Equation: 100 Factors that Can Add or Subtract Years from Your Life.* Avon, MA.: Adams Media, 2007.

Marchione, Marilyn. *'Exercise Is a Drug' That's Addicting Older America.* Cincinnati Enquirer, May 15, 2014, p. D3.

Masley, Steven. *Ten Years Younger: The Amazing Ten-Week Plan to Look Better, Feel Better and Turn Back the Clock*. New York: Broadway Books, 2005.

Mayo Clinic. *Mayo Clinic Heart Healthy for Life: The Mayo Clinic Plan for Preventing and Conquering Heart Disease*. New York: Time Home Entertainment Corporation Inc., 2012.

Mayo Clinic Staff, Healthy Lifestyle - Adult Health, *Napping: Do's and Don'ts for Healthy Adults*,

McFarland, Judy Lindberg. *Aging without Growing Old*. Lake Mary, FL: Siloam Press, 2003.

McGraw, Robin. *What's Age Got to do with It?* Nashville: Thomas Nelson, 2009.

Mercola, Joseph. *Artificial Sweeteners Can Trigger Cancer*. Mercola.com, March 30, 2016.

Mercola, Joseph. *Artificial Sweeteners Cause Greater Weight Gain than Sugar*. Mercola.com, December 4, 2012.

Metler, Molly and Kemper, Donald W. *Healthwise for Life: A Medical Self-Care Guide for You (8th Edition)*. Boise, Idaho: Healthwise, 2011.

Mozaffarian, Dariush. Ed. *Fruits and Vegetables Linked to Better Weight Control: Substituting for Other Foods Can Improve Long-Term Weight Control*. Health and Nutrition Letter, January 2016, pp.1-2.

National Center for Health Statistics. *Mortality in the United States, 2015.* cdc.gov>nchs

Nava, Coach Dan. *Fit After 40: 3 Keys to Looking Great and Feeling Great.* Nashville: Thomas Nelson, Inc., 2006.

Neal, Katie. *Forever Young: Your Chances of Celebrating your 100th Birthday Are Better Than Ever. Now What?* Parade, January 22, 2017, pp. 311-313

Ni, Mao Shing. *Secrets of Longevity: Hundreds of Ways to Live to Be 100.* San Francisco: Chronicle Books, 2006.

Null, Gary. *Gary Null's Power Aging.* New York: New American Library, 2003.

O'Brien, Mary. *Successful Aging.* Concord, CA.: Biomed General, 2007.

Ornish, Dean. *The Spectrum: A Scientifically Proven Program to Feel Better, Live Longer, Lose Weight and Gain Health.* New York: Ballantine Books, 2007.

Oz, Mehmet, and Roizen, Michael F., with Spiker, Ted, Wynett, Craig, Oz, Lisa, and Rudberg, Mark A., *You Staying Young: The Owner's Manual for Extending Your Warranty.* New York: Free Press, 2007.

Patchell-Evans, David. *Living the Good Life: Your Guide to Health and Success.* Toronto, Ontario: ECW Press, 2001.

Perls, Thomas T. & Silver, Margery Hutter with Lauerman, John F. *Living to 100: Lessons in Living to Your Maximum Potential at Any Age*. New York: Basic Books, 1999.

Perricone, Nicholas. *7 Secrets to Beauty, Health and Longevity: The Miracle of Cellular Rejuvenation*. New York: Ballantine Books, 2006.

Plasker, Eric, *The 100 Year Lifestyle: Workout*. Guilford, Connecticut: Globe Pequot Press, 2010.

Plasker, Eric, *The 100 Year Lifestyle*. Avon, MA: Adams Media, 2007.

Powers, Scott K. & Dodd, Stephen L. *Total Fitness and Wellness*. New York: Custom Publishing, 2009.

Reyes, Mandel. *The Healing Power of Humor*. Kansas City, Mo: United Healthcare, Winter, 2017, pp. 17-19.

Rippe, James M. *High Performance Health: 10 Real Life Solutions to Redefine Your Health*. Nashville: Thomas Nelson, 2007.

Rippe, James M. *Workbook High Performance Health: 10 Real Life Solutions to Redefine Your Health*. Nashville: Thomas Nelson, 2007.

Rippe, James M. *Your Plan for a Balanced Life*. Nashville: Thomas Nelson, 2008.

Roizen, M.D., Michael F. *The Real Age Makeover: Take Years Off Your Looks and Add Them to*

Your Life. New York: Harper Collins Publishers Inc., 2004.

Rosen, Michael W. *100 Smart Choices: Easy Ideas for Living Healthier and Happier*. Emmaus PA: Rodale Press, 2008.

Rosenberg, Irwin H. Ed. *Staying Active and Social Prolongs Life Even After 75: Exercise Is the Number-One Contributor to Longevity*. Health and Nutrition Letter: Your Guide to Living Healthier Longer, Volume 13G, p.3.

Rosenberg, Irwin H. Ed. *Healthy Diet and Lifestyle Help Prevent Disability in Aging*. Health and Nutrition Letter, November 2013, p.3.

Rosenberg, Irwin H. Ed. *Protein Plus Exercise Equals Less Muscle Loss with Aging: Over 50? You May Not Be Getting Enough Protein*. Health and Nutrition Letter, June 2014, p.7.

Rowe, John W. and Kahn, Robert L. *Successful Aging*. New York: Dell Publishing, 1998.

Rubin, Jordan with Remedios, David. *The Great Physician's RX for Health and Wellness: Seven Keys to Unlocking Your Health Potential*. Nashville, TN.: Nelson Books, 2005.

Scarmo, Stephanie. *Exercising the Truth: What Works? What Doesn't?*, Nutrition Action, January/February 2014, pp. 9-11.

Schardt, David and Scarmo, Stephanie. *Multi Dilemma: Should You Take One?* Nutrition Action Health Letter, November 2013, pp.3-7.

Schardt, David. *Walk This Way, Please: 7 Reasons to Lace Up Your Sneakers.* Nutrition Action, Letter: Your Guide to Living Longer, Special Supplement, September 2014.

Schwarzbein, Diana and Deville, Nancy. *The Schwarzbein Principle: The Truth About Losing Weight, Being Healthy and Feeling Younger.* Deerfield Beach, FL: Health Communications, Inc., 1999.

Shealy, C. Norman. *Life Beyond 100: Secrets of the Fountain of Youth.* New York: Jeremy P. Tarcher/Penguin, 2005.

Somers, Suzanne. *Breakthrough: 8 Steps to Wellness: Life-Altering Secrets from Today's Cutting-Edge Doctors.* New York: Three Rivers Press, 2008.

Sternberg, Barbara. Pet Therapy: *Therapeutic Effect of Pets.* Institute for Natural Resources, Home Study #2380, June 2009.

Sternberg, Barbara. *Humor and Healing.* Institute for Natural Resources, Home Study #2390, July 2009.

Storrs, Carina. *The Centarian Tide is on the Rise.* CNN Health, January 25, 2016.

Thomas, John. *Young Again: How to Reverse the Aging Process*, 6th Edition. Mead, WA.: Plexus Press, 2006.

Traver, Kelly & Sargent, Betty Kelly. *The Program: The Brain-Smart Approach to the Healthiest You*. New York: Atria Books, 2009.

Vaillant, George E. *Aging Well*. New York: Little, Brown and Company, 2002.

Weil, Andrew. *Healthy Aging: A Lifelong Guide to Your Well-Being*. New York: Anchor Books, 2007.

West Virginia Department of Health and Human Resources, *Obesity: Facts, Figures and Guidelines*.

Winerman, Lea. *A Healthy Mind, A Longer Life: Can the Right Attitude and Personality Help You Live Longer? Psychologists Are Trying to Find Out*. Monitor on Psychology, November 2006, pp.42-44.

ENDNOTES

1. Fossanden, Marissa, Smithsonian.com, January 22, 2016.
2. Storrs, Carina, CNN Health, January 25, 2016.
3. Perls, Thomas T., Silver, Margery Hutter with Lauterman, John F., p.17.
4. Howard, Michael E., p.13.
5. Evans-Pritchard, Ambrose, Telegraph, January 20, 2016.
6. Howard, Michael E., p. 129.
7. CDC Fact Sheet, Fast Facts – Smoking and Tobacco Use, Updated March 29, 2017.
8. Ibid.
9. O'Brien, Mary, p.40.
10. Fred Hutchinson Cancer Research Center, Just One Alcoholic Drink a Day Increases Breast Cancer Risk; Exercise Lowers Risk, May 23, 2017.
11. Mercola.com, Artificial Sweeteners, October 3, 2017 and December 4, 2012.
12. National Center for Health Statistics, Mortality in the United States 2015.
13. Weil, Andrew, p.234.
14. Flanigan, Richard J. and Flanigan Sawyer, Kate, p.70.
15. Wvdhhr.org, Obesity: Facts, Figures and Guidelines.
16. Berlin, Irving, Song Count Your Blessings Instead of Sheep.
17. Mayo Clinic Staff, Healthy Lifestyle Adult Health, Napping Do's and Don'ts.
18. Liponis, MarK, pp. 81-226.

19. Flanigan, Richard J., and Flanigan Sawyer, Kate, p. 96.
20. O'Brien, Mary, p.106.
21. Judge, Kandeel, Barish-Wreden, Maxine and Brees, Karen, p. 117.
22. Flanigan, Richard J., and Flanigan Sawyer, Kate, p. 95
23. Ibid., p.96
24. Mayo Clinic Plan, pp.106-107.
25. Rippe, James, p. 20.
26. Perls, Thomas T., Silver, Margery Hutter with Lauterman, John F., p. 77.
27. CDC.gov, Depression – Data Sources; Depression Statistics, 2005-2006.
28. Dylan, Bob. Song – These Times They Are A-Changin.
29. Rippe, James, p.148
30. Mayo Clinic Plan, p.111.
31. Judge, Kandeel, Barish-Wreden, Maxine and Brees, Karen, p.121.
32. Giampapa, Vincent, Pero, Ronald and Zimmerman, Marcia, p.42
33. Judge, Kandeel, Barish-Wreden, Maxine and Brees, Karen, pp.260-261.

YOUR AUTHOR

Admiral Sanders is 80 years old with 40 years' experience as a psychologist and 27 years serving weekends as a pastor in mostly small churches. He has completed 82 full marathons, 5 of which were at age 79. In 2004, he walked across the USA at age 67 fulfilling a dream that began 50 years earlier. For almost two years after that, he searched for a new sense of purpose. Eventually there was the sense that he was to be a role model for those coming behind, those who needed some future direction from someone who was already there. At first that seemed arrogant, but that feeling was followed by the realization that all of us rely on older role models to show us the way. Now he is still working 3 days per week, has a personal trainer, attends Weight Watchers weekly and is involved in church and community activities.

ACKNOWLEDGEMENTS

This book was not the work of just one person but was completed with the invaluable support of many people. Many different colleagues and friends were asked to read or edit the book to help it stay true to the primary purpose of providing as much information related to healthy aging that could be included in a book that someone could read in approximately 60 minutes. This book is dedicated to my wife, Dorothy Sanders. She was the first and perhaps most important supporter as she read the first rough draft and made recommendations for important changes. She also was supportive in allowing the author the freedom to work together instead of spending relaxed time as a family.

Dr. Kimberly Sanders and Dr. Craig Sanders made some important contributions to this book based on their experience in their medical practices and their passion to live healthy and happy lives.

Dr. Ann Crowe and Dr, Phyllis Kramer were the two persons who edited the book. Dr. Kramer was the one who edited to first "final draft" and made many changes that helped the book present many ideas in a way that was easier to understand for the reader. Dr. Crowe did the final editing before the book was formatted for publication. She also made many key suggestions for changes. Without the help of these two persons, the book lacked the clarity and brevity necessary for helping the readers plan important changes. Barbara Mullins' help was invaluable as she designed the cover and did all the formatting required for an e-book and a paperback. Her help in complying with all required formatting by the publisher allowed to book to finally be published.

John McIntire and Lindsey McIntire also provided recommendations and suggested changes that were extremely important. Their own work in research related to health and wellness made the authors aware of advances in the field that improved accuracy. Finally, many others read the book and made comments including Judine M. Hooker, Kellie Shumate, Dierdra Robison, Mike Kramer, Amanda Kramer and Sherre Hall. Our thanks to all who helped move this project to completion.

Made in the USA
Middletown, DE
08 September 2019